My 100 Greatest Moments

OOR WULLIE®

My 100 Greatest Moments

BLACK & WHITE PUBLISHING

First published 2017
by Black & White Publishing Ltd
104 Commercial Street, Edinburgh, EH6 6NF

1 3 5 7 9 10 8 6 4 2   17 18 19 20

ISBN: 978 1 910230 45 9

Oor Wullie ® © DC Thomson & Co. Ltd. 2017
Text by Iain McLaughlin

A CIP catalogue record for this book is available from
the British Library.

Typeset by Creative Link, North Berwick
Printed and bound by Opolgraf, Poland

Introduction

For over eighty years, Scotland's favourite wee scamp has been making mischief and causing mayhem, bringing countless smiles along the way. This is a collection of Wullie's one hundred favourite moments, in no particular order, picked by the wee rogue himself.

Pull up a bucket and join the fun.

1. I used brains instead o' muscle in the gairden!

2. I wis so guid at gowf, I got
the cup afore I left the
gowf shop!

3. I'm champion berry picker o' a' Auchenshoogle . . .

But I'm also champion berry eater o' a' Auchenshoogle!

4. I worked oot my career plan guid an' early.

5. I learnt hoo tae get a free
read o' a comic, jist by being
taller than a wee lad.

6. My best ever mischief-makin' disguise!

7. I found a right unusual way o' takin' Mrs McGurk's dug for a walk.

8. I found sheep tae coont so I could fall asleep . . .

There's ay a rascal tae
wak ye up, though!

9. I turned the West Sands intae the Wild West . . .

I'm a real Jock Wayne!

10. This is ane o' my worst moments. Actually, it's been dozens o' my worst moments. My pals are ay gettin' me in trouble.

11. I'm no' a bad lad really.
I gave this fella my
ma last 5p.

12. The time I became my pals' hero by knockin' oot Bully Benson . . .

They didnae ken he knocked
himself oot tryin' tae
get in my shed!

13. When me an' my pals a' wanted thon racin' car fae the toy shop . . .

And I had ither pals wha saw me
'icht wi' something even better!

14. I mind Ma sayin'
I'd never mak' onything
of the bagpiping . . .

But I made a fortune
scarin' the craws!

15. I got a rare bite at
Stoorie Burn!

16. My best dream ever – putting Bob an' Soapy in their place!

17. I invented central heatin'. It's a Fact!

All ye need is a couple o' bricks,
a wee candle an' a bucket.

18. I became a champion Hielan' dancer . . .

An' I wasnae even tryin'!

19. Move ower Rabbie Burns – this laddie's a real poet!

20. The Auchenshoogle
Championship of draughts - held
in the library so Bob couldnae
gloat too loud when he won.

21. The best way to win the
Easter Egg race is to eat
your egg first and then roll it.

22. If you're going to get caught fishing where you shouldnae, make sure it's where PC Murdoch does his fishing.

23. The time I accidentally playe
leapfrog wi' PC Murdoch when
trying to catch my budgie!

24. The best feeling in the world – bringing a smile to Ma's face. I'm an awfy crawler.

25. I wish somebody had telt
me the double bass wasnae
jist a muckle great fiddle.

26. The day I won the World's
Messiest Bedroom Award -
according to Ma.

27. Ma made a clootie
dumpling and I had tae go
to the hospital . . .

MUMBLE-MUMBLE-THREE INCHES ALONG FROM HAT BIG CURRANT AN'--

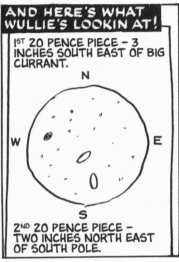

AND HERE'S WHAT WULLIE'S LOOKIN AT!

1ST 20 PENCE PIECE - 3 INCHES SOUTH EAST OF BIG CURRANT.

N

W   E

S

2ND 20 PENCE PIECE - TWO INCHES NORTH EAST OF SOUTH POLE.

An X-ray was the only way tae find out where the coins were!

28. Pa's chair is perfect to gie
a laddie his best sleep ever.

29. Have ye ever seen a rollerskating dug afore?

30. This wisnae my cleverest idea – using a hair drier to cool Pa's lunch got me – and him – in the soup.

31. I joined up to be a sojer and protect Auchenshoogle and Bonnie Scotland!

32. Ma tells me tae eat mair fruit – well, this ice cream has raspberry syrup on it!

33. Ma wondered how I got top marks in the test at school – I'm no' tellin'!

34. Did ye ken that it only taks a torch tae turn you into a monster?

35. I broke Usain Bolt's record for the 100 metres – when a muckle big coo chased me!

36. Even long walks are good fun tae a laddie like me.

37. My auntie might dress me like a wee bairn but she's the best fighter in oor toon!

38. Winner (and only competitor)
o' the Auchenshoogle
Mr Universe contest.

39. I've ay said ye cannae beat
   a cup of tea - or at least a
   ~ight big teapot to fill wi' water.

40. I showed aff my best
manners to auld Miss McLean . .

It's jist a pity her ain
manners are gye rough!

41. I'll be wi ye' in a minute – a'thing stops for tatties and mince!

42. Bob and me invented the daftest way to ride horses!

43. The best way to avoid getting' booked for hand ball? Be a goalie!

44. Winning a talent contest wi'
a dancin' dug? Auchenshoogle's
Got Talent did it first!

45. It's an awfy thing tae discover yer faither's a big feartie when he taks ye campin'

46. I made a fortune wi' my shoeshine business at the circus – I charged by the inch!

47. I mind I souped up my cartie
dog power is faster than
horse power!

48. I used my head to get a job on a building site.

49. I only missed oot on an Olympic javelin medal because I got disqualified for haein' a man's nose on the end.

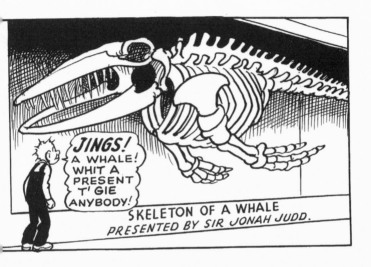

50. My best ever catch at the Fishing was a whopper.
(Aye, Wullie, and so's this claim!)

51. A dug might be a man's best friend . . .

But a hot dog is a hungry
laddie's best friend!

52. It's braw to hae a cousin who looks jist like me – Ma can only tell us apart because he washes his neck better.

53. When I got rested by my Fitba team I was the physio - and I soon opened up a place in the team!

54. Santie Claus always kens if
I've been naughty or nice –
but brings me toys onyway!

55. What's the best day in the world?
A mud-fight wi' your best pals.

56. It's a weird day when the law
asks you tae knock their helmet
aff – aff a branch, that is!

57. Best place for a sneaky
snooze ever? Ma's pulley
is jist braw.

58. Faithers are a' sadists –
jist because they're losin' their
hair they mak' sure we lose
ours regularly!

9. Dinnae eat cheese afore bed.
I gied my bucket weird looks
for days after I did.

60. Pa telt me I should ay help if
I see somebody in trouble . . .

But nae good deed
goes unpunished.

61. I "said it wi' flowers"
on Mother's Day – and I got
some rare mince and
doughballs in return!

62. Bob telt me to hae just
one piece o' pie . . . so I did!

63. I'm a dab hand wi' a violin. I cannae play a tune but my forehand is braw.

64. How to earn a couple of quid guid and quick. Take up duck-walking. All ye need is an auld car horn.

65. A lesson to a' laddies –
pet hedgehogs and Pas
dinnae ay mix!

66. I found the very job for me – teachin' cartie driving!

67. Ay be kind tae animals – like
when I replaced the coats the
fermer sheared aff the sheep.

8. If you're skint, ask to try the toys before you buy onything. Ye can play wi' a'thing in the shop for nae money.

69. It's an awfy thing when
fowk mak fun o' your gloves . .

There are some gloves they
dinnae laugh at sae much!

70. When it comes tae pinchin' cakes, a wee pet moose is a laddie's best friend!

71. I'm official champion o' balancin' a barrel on my heid. Naebody else entered the contest. Weird that.

72. Have ye ever been tae an art exhibition? I'd have got detention if I drew this kind o' stuff for art class!

73. I thought PC Murdoch had lost the plot when somebody said he was wearing a bear skin – turns oot he was a sojer.

74. When your Ma says you can only hae one drink o' juice, make sure it's a big bottle!

5. I invented a braw new game –
rollerskate Fitba. I'm lightnin'
Fast on the wing.

76. It's a terrible thing
to get your name taken
by PC Murdoch . . .

But it's braw to get your ain
back when you're referee in his
game o' fitba!

77. I invented a braw way of makin' Wee Eck no sae wee!

78. I wis sad tae miss Bob, but I hit an even better target!

79. Never inspect anither man's bucket withoot askin' first. It ca cause an awfy sore bahookie!

80. Wha needs Ben Hur?
A' ye need is a chair on wheels
an' a big dug wantin' a walk.

81. I didnae hit any high notes but I hit a high heid. Big Tam wisnae pleased!

82. Never ever play fitba
against a lampie –
they're big dirty cheats!

83. PC Murdoch was a real
blowhard tellin' me how
to tak a photae . . .

But my photae o' him was a
bit too natural for him!

84. I'm a man o' words but this happens when I find oot I have to dance wi' lassies!

5. Have you ever wondered whit cowboys would be like if they were around the day? A different kind o' horse power!

86. Abody wis impressed with my magic show, when I sawed Wee Eck in half - they didnae realise there were twa boys in the box!

87. Have ye never heard the
phrase "like a bull in a
furniture shop"?!

88. There's nothing as pleasin' as being able to jump the Shallow Burn an' win the Auchenshoogle long jump contest . . .

Except seeing Bully Briggs
no' jump it!

BLA-A-AH,
I'M NO'
PAYIN' FOR
THAT MUCK!

89. My lemonade recipe wisnae the greatest success!

90. That time I mistook cod liver oil for suntan oil!

91. The teacher telt us to keep a scrap book...

She didnae have this kind of
scrap in mind!

92. This auld lad's hilarious method for growin' a beard!

93. We pirates o' the High Street
    flegged auld Murdoch . . .

A' it needed was a model boat
and a smart lad on skates.

94. My career as a hairdresser
wis short-lived!

95. I treated Ma tae a really posh meal – wi' a difference!

96. A library is a richt guid place
to go on a rainy afternoon . . .

You ay get a smart idea
or twa there!

97. It's fair excitin' to find a polis box in Auchenshoogle . . .

And a bit disappointin' tae find
it's nae Doctor Who – jist
PC Murdoch eatin' a jeely piece.

98. The awfy moment when you realise you've got a geography test in school . . .

But then you realise you ken all
the answers from the names of
fitba teams.

99. I Found a way of makin' it look as if I'm studying really hard in class!

100. I started a fashion
craze for a while . . .

But abody kens there's only one Oor Wullie!